NOVEMBER 1ST AVENUE

POETRY BY APRIL

NOVEMBER 1ST AVENUE

BY APRIL

To my younger sister whose art is scattered all over this book To me
To you

The contents

November 1st Avenue

Lonely streets and haunted gas stations I walked down the avenue all alone
And that's when I knew
That the street lights are only bright when I look at them And my eyes only
hurt when I think of you

Orange Green And red

Street lights to guide me through
Red like the lake you held my head under just because you wondered How it
felt to be a God
Orange like the sunsets we watched through a livestream of your eternal
smoke and self loathe
And green like my eyes as you joked about the black holes in the center And
how wide they were for a regular girl
That is what you called me What you thought of me
But the birds at 6.06 told me otherwise They sang for me for hours!
Flapped their fucking wings around me to breathe better
They told me the wise pine tree remembered me from when I was only eleven
Telling her ghostly leaves how bad I want to leave
Hug the greenery in my eyes
And break free of my father's chains
You told me I was a regular Just like my father did
And how obedient and silent my mother was And for that, my old friend
I do not love you anymore

شارع
أول نوفمبر
AVENUE DU
1er NOVEMBRE

Women

Women They have minds

And they have souls, as well as just hearts
And they've got ambition and they've got talent
As well as just beauty
I'm so sick of people saying that love is all a woman is fit for I'm so sick of it
I'm so sick of marriage proposals and picnics
In hushed laughter

I'm so sick of it Women are loud and fierce Women are quiet and
gentle

Women are stubborn and creative Women are romantic and humble
Women leave notes under your pillow once they're done playing Playing games
in a man's world
Where they're told to speak quietly and less often
Shrug prejudice mindlessly and sheepishly Smile and smile with white teeth
Women now have finish lines
They must meet the finish line with their male equals Yet the finish line is
always running up
Hills of jokes about skirts and scarfs Hair and tattoos
Weight and sins
Hills of southern anger and of steep unfairness Women
They have minds
And they have souls as well as just hearts

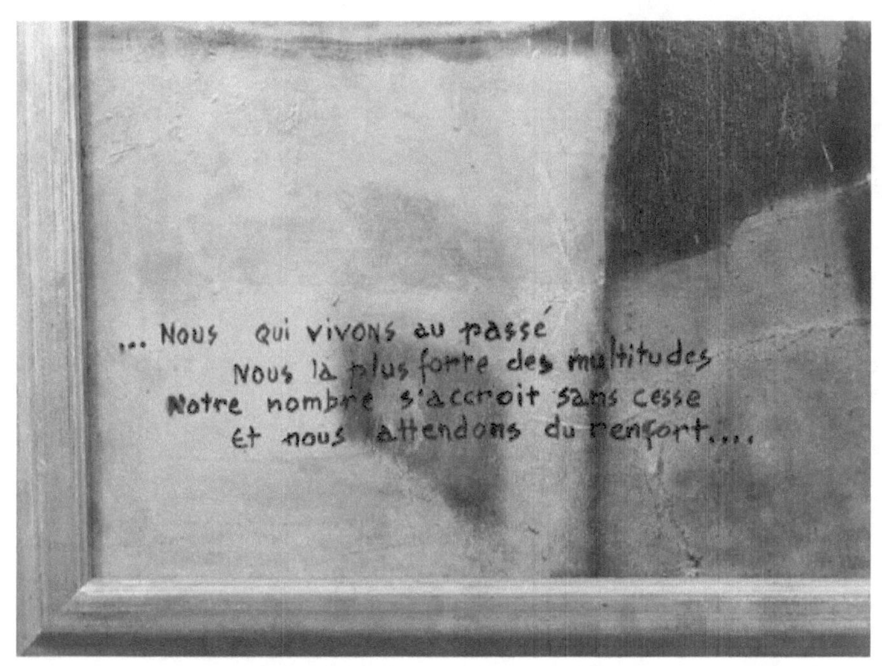
... Nous qui vivons au passé
Nous la plus forte des multitudes
Notre nombre s'accroit sans cesse
Et nous attendons du renfort....

My mother

My mother is sixty years young
She is beautiful, young of the time at least Did not age like wine, but rather like water In an
endless cycle of patience and patience Her dreams, not a puddle, but rather an ocean A pound,
uncared for in nineteen sixty-two When her waters were spit on and defiles Her ocean, artless
and green with mold
A puddle evaporated on her wedding night When she met my father for the first time
Her heart must have skipped beats and organs failed The creator of her ocean
Drowned in normality and broken dreams So her daughters write about her pains Wonder if
she was ever afraid
And wanted her mommy to tuck her in
A dreadful cruel fate she was promised
Her patience never thin, forevermore
It rained at times, smiles and lonesome farewells
To cracked ribs and lonesome nights
Yet, the shame resides eyes
In her newly acquainted and shivering lies
Th puddle, the pound, the ocean
Swept away along the sixty years of dread
The puddle, the pound, the ocean
Dry, yet clean of salt and mold
The waters are gone but the spirit lives on
Maybe in me, or maybe in the mountains
Where she was born

Me-shaped grenades

Me-shapes grenades thrown at me My own brown eyes and dark jokes My own
sour skin and salty eyes My own naive heart
Your bitter hands A friend
My friend my ally
My right hand my foe's foe
Me shapes grenades
Is it really you scheming and whispering my name Or my arrogance that
provokes?
Every bit Every parcel Every ash
Of my unwavering arrogance My absolutes and nevers
My commitment to spoken truths and white lies I am ashamed of myself when
I hear your voice Here I sit again in this embarrassment this decay In my own
sweat and tears

In the remnants of what we used to be What about the American
dream and biology

Algerian women's rights, our rights Where everything is notions Guesses
And assumptions
But you shall never know my address and phone number You shall forever be a
stranger
Someone A stranger
An acquaintance A friend
An acquaintance A stranger
Someone I don't know
My other half would never tremor My love would never

Normality

My limbs move as I command them to They go as I imagine them to move
Though they live in utter obedience Never disconnect or call me a liar
Their refusal to follow was torn or tearing As on the beach, a dazzling view
The waters so warm, my parts let go A dream it is or reality
They don't know, they take it for a fantasy
The water washes over me Dissolve every dirt in my pores And turn it into gold
Cleanse my hair from all my emotional headaches And still, they refuse to swim to shore
My limbs move as I command them to Except today, reality is the shoreline
And my fantasy is the sea
Maybe my body knows I belong in the sky A star my loved ones mourn
Look up to the sunset and await me to luminesce And recall the day my body never swam to shore How it loosened my hold on life
On every hope I wrote at fifteen

Command me to be good

Consider this letter my polite goodbye Begging you, lord
To command me to be good
Oh, what I would do to have them call me Ordinary and unremarkable
Typical and unreliable I know everyone can see
The purple smudged under my hazed eyes Yet they call me a fucking prize
God, I tried though I tried so hard to
Wine and dine my father's sick need to undermine
To swallow my vomit and smile Smile smile smile and smile a little more
But I'm no beautiful fool I've always known
That I was smarter than my cousin Smarter than his brother and mine That I
will be taking care of me
Like the bees I trapped in a plastic bottle Collecting them like my baby teeth
Teeth I lost when I was seven springs and eight summers
To my brother's drug use
I'm falling fast to my knees
To my doom Command me to be a fool
Like my mother and her mother before her Bees buzzing with life inside a
plastic bottle

Toughen up, little girl

Disarm me
Unbuckle my head and heart, slowly slowly Take my neurons and leave
Suck the anger out of my ears
I do want to implode and say fuck them men Once a day
Once a week Once a month
Tell me I can't cause I was born sick
I was born sick and you punish me for it You punish us for it
You suppress my clever jokes and my divergent opinions It scares you that I am
a woman, doesn't it?
I am less and he is the most
He gets more and more for being born blooming A man oh man

Oh, to be a strong man Never forced to do any of this

Tutor my anger and tailor my time Tailor my life and step up my work Step up
my art and quicken my journey
Quicken my wits and better my judgment Better my money and slow my pace
Slow my heart and engage my voice Engage my thoughts and break a smile
Break a sweat and enjoy my fire
Enjoy my girlhood and toughen my skin Toughen up, little girl
Toughen up

October

Was it October? Or was it the wind?

I flattened my narrative and my truth Spilled lonesome in my ocean
of anger and despise

My staged fights and rehearsed talks

With the mulberry tree that abandoned me in my fright Yet I died
I died with wings and no courage to fly Dreams of New York and Amsterdam
Cracked my spine beneath the unaligned stars
That sunk into the earths and skinned my teeth and nails
And my toys I stole from my friend's friend Were buried under the dust of my
disobedience And under the ruins of everything
I died, but was never reborn With 77 unfinished selves Drowned futures
And forgotten red promises
That were veiled my plagued periphery And I spit me out

I spit me out and never grieved the loss of me Nothing goes rogue in
October Except the raging angry wind

That unearthed our tree from the roots And my love for me with it

Mania

My lover clings to his sheet in pain
As I dissect his heart strings and dissolve his brains in my anger His tears are
dry and cries are muffled
I burst into flames and burnt his hand Reaching out to hold me
And I live in an old ghost town where our tree is still dancing with the wind
As the leaves sing all night and day
It's so strange, large hysteria leaving his veins Hysteria is my ghost friend from
when I was nine Hysteria, my drug that keeps him awake at night Even the
awls sleep
But my baby never sleeps
Awaiting mania to cloudburst through my mouth when I'm mad And I'm
mad all life long

And when the torture is over My lover goes to the sleep clinic Where
no fix is hysterical or manic

Not like me Never like me

Or my sharp decision cutting through his artery And will he stay? If
I dare to ask him to stay In the mezzanine between heaven and hell

Between endless battles And sweet love making
Cause, lover, if I could change my name
I'd call me Mania

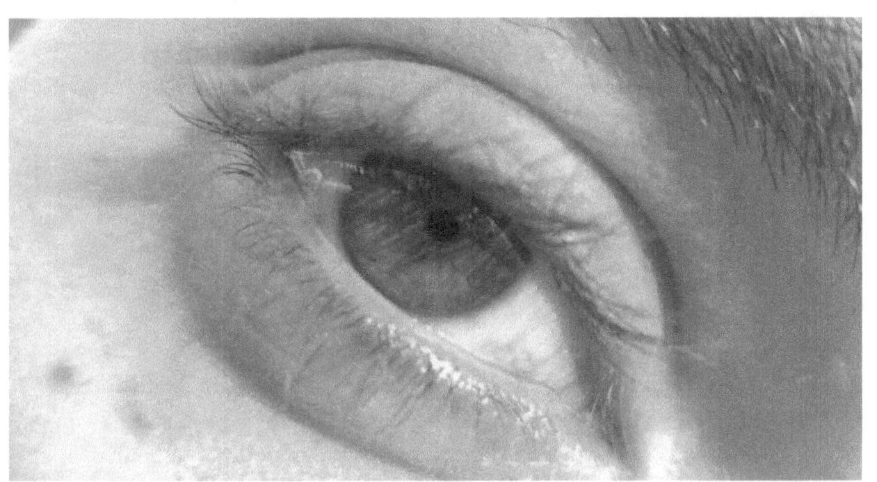

I always waited anxiously for trains

Fear of trains and summers
Opposites, yet in my head they're the same
Exhausted in dreams I roam my station
Staring at the horizon, my vision doubles and the lines between what's real and what's fake
blur

SummerSummer Summer

Your sun reigns high in the sky but my father hates the light And so do I
But at 9.10AM I hear your horns singing for a glorious arrival People run and swim in your
wings and crown you their king But my sweat is moldy and spoiled
And my skin sheds years of velvet puberty
You won't like me, Mr cold breeze
Mr happy underneath the palm trees
Your Majesty,
I wait anxiously for the trains at the station

By the homeless who sell tissues for a penny and a half They wear sweaters with holes
in their pockets and unbrushed hair

Organic eyes and stolen dreams And in my fantasy, I tell them
"I want to hold you, take you and sweep your skin
Away from trains and summers"
But sometimes I just wish I could do that for me too I know this is a metaphor no one
comprehends
But maybe someday, someone shall

11 hearts

You have bleached my heart and nails And I see you more often now
By the sea

By the mighty port In the heart of Algiers The heart of my heart

Calloused fingertips and chipped hearts Breathe in the poison of
cars and angry smokers

The heart of my heart Stupid stupid love Stupid stupid heart
A stricken heart with wrath and wrath
An incandescent love shown the sloppiest slopes above Drink and play
Walk and crawl Run
But rise
Rise between the untouched and the ungranted Mine mine believe
Mine mine believe The heart of my heart
Believe me and my soulless poetry My loveless hugs
My bleached lips Colorless eyes Mine mine love Mine oh mine love Love me
A lonesome path within strings of denial Denial of a mind, a joyous mind
Mine mine gift Mine mine gift
Gift me forgetfulness of my mother, her wounds
My father, his wounding

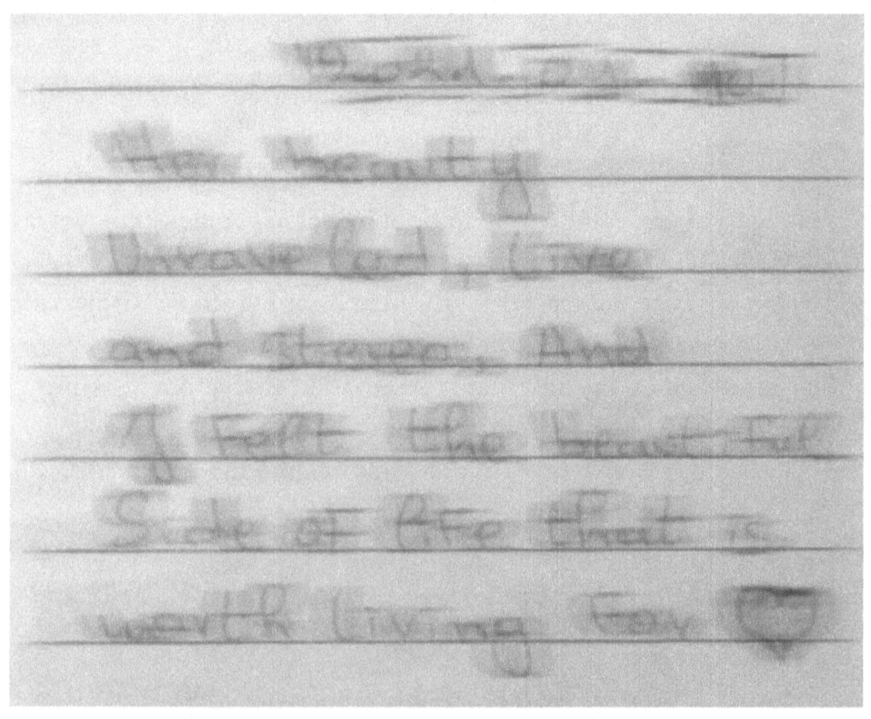
World and her
Her beauty
Unraveled, Lives
and Stevee. And
I felt the beautiful
Side of life that is
worth living for

My body?

I wish to own my body My only home
Locally made by two unloving beings But who am I fooling really?
Why am I lying to myself?
That cannot happen Not now and not ever
For so long I've been a wandering spirit Spitting on people's unmown lawn
Pores too large, they could fit an ocean
An ocean of sweat and tears from running Running after a faithless life
A life of joyless hair and makeup Perfume and cologne
Skin stretched on my hips that I used to hide Too fat or too skinny
Which is it today?
Uneven eyes in the shape of almonds
Or at least that's what I've been told

An almond the size of earth and the space Spearing towards my humped back and crooked teeth

Everywhere is unsafe My body is not safe
If I paint my nails, I'm a whore
If I laugh a little loud, I'm unworthy If I sleep too much, I'm unfit
And what if I die?
If I die, my body is back to dust

First time, is that okay?

Come hangout with me by the mulberry tree

I'm on my bruised knees at 13 years Don't stare at my hair, the hole
in my socks

Or the cockroach in my mouth I had mistaken it for a berry
A ripe burgundy berry
Everyone laughed but it wasn't funny
I promise your hair won't fall all, not at first Don't worry, my friend
Young girls die too Young boys die too
Even if you don't smoke or even try
A frameless window the size of my Christian friend's bible
One two three four five Rinse, repeat
One two three four five Rinse repeat
Water drips on the floor
My Marlboro and lips touch just for me to cough And cough a little more
Should I jump? You think?
The grass looks forest green from my angle I swear
But don't count on my words, I haven't worn my glasses for two months
Sixteen days One hour
And two seconds, three four five Rinse
Repeat

Picnics on the moon

Flowers on the bench where I used to sit with my high school friends Staring
at the rug that hugs the grass and covers its greenery
And what a scenery
A pathway made to heaven

Or what they call the Mediterranean Sea Bees buzzing with life,
giving life and taking fear

They're violet and violent Swimming in air just like I do Can you hear the
music?
It's calling on me to be beautiful
And I sit and laugh with my mother on my mind Mania clutching my brains
that spill on my teal skin Afraid if i don't cherish the moment it's forever lost
In an ocean of forgetfulness
Afraid I'd never smile again
My picnics on the moon never last long
I am infinitely too many concepts and personas Too many emotions hopes and
dreams Different cuts of different colors and shapes Sewn together
And I wear me everywhere
I love love nature and humans And talks and walks around places
I love love yellow books that speaks of Roman choirs and Islamic triumphs
But they seclude me in godless womb
And fatherless guards

My theatrics

Nose touching the ceiling Hands behind your back In other words
You are an arrogant and a dangerous woman A dangerous woman they call
you
But all you think about is your childhood memories They spread like wildfire
for a little while
Wildfire in your backyard while you say goodbye to Winter you
Summer you Poor you
Gardens and lakes
Pretty flowers and pretty waters Blue irises and blue boardwalks Green grass
and green mold Swift winds and swift splashes Floating bees and floating
plastic Beautiful gardens
I am sorry you are embarrassed to write I am sorry you love your poetry
And other do not
I am sorry all are quick to forsake your daring remarks Arrogant
Arrogant
My arrogance my theatrics
A theatre for my peers and professors Family and ancestors
In a house like my ego, always breaks And one relief for the arrogant
One freedom
The freedom of death, oblivion

Gemini science

I can teach you how to bewitch the mind And ensnare the senses
I can tell you how to bottle fame Brew glory
And even put a stopper in death
I can teach you how to speak in ancient tongues And riddle the clever
I can tell you how to gather answers Pluck luck
And even water the pain
I can teach you how to seduce the wise And make their acquaintance
Slow cook your schemes And even guide the blind And when all fails
When it fails to be good Which it undoubtedly will
I can teach you how to steal hearts And lie eye to eye
Smile to a dying face
And dance on unmarked graves
I can teach you how to blanket your fears with the sun And charm your
nemesis to death
Our nemesis
I can slow your death
And mine

I know God loves me cause I write

Seagulls in Algiers
Seagulls nesting on mosques and in my hair Everyone falling in love with
'Merica
For the *American Dream*
But everyone is kind in Algiers
The teeming thoroughfares and the remainder of the French written all over
the buildings
Where boys and boys tell me "When God made you, he took his time"
But everyone is kind in Algiers
Have my seat please I didn't wake up at 5AM Have my mittens please it's not
that cold Overzealous smiles

Thrifted clothes and thrifted morals From the colonizers to my great
grandfather

To then my great grandmother All the way to me
All the long way to vain little me Watering a plastic rose in my hair To appear
kind and well

But I was born sick in East Algiers Buses and autumn Autumn and
winter
Winter and music Music and you

Plastic roses on my grave

Give me grace please
Be patient with my bones creaking
And my skin cracking like the Sahara in July and august

Yes, I know I'm young But I'm well aware of the odds

Of me reaching Mars when water is back
I'm young but my grave is a chamber of secrets and hypocrisy
A slippery slope, one would never hope That the school ghosts were right
And oh, what I wouldn't give to be discovered
I am a con artist; I am a fraud in plain sight So please
Pay your respects in my wake
Walk in with plastic roses and an earthquake Then I might awake
But the ravens knew of your clownlike heart That lowly me had never seen
And lowly me had never seen
A kept all-night vigil beside my death bed My mother never did
Plastics bags Plastics roses
Accumulating my jokes and odd remarks

Fraud

I'm tired of carrying my hands around My scarred and scorned limbs
Survival of the fittest, the smartest and the luckiest Survival of the luckiest and
you know it
Survival of the ones with better parents than mine and yours and you know it
But we pretend to not know and try
Fuck our way up to the top
Lie and trick the lucky weak that we are alike Dinners on time and Harvard at
eighteen

I left my hometown back in October 2018 And *it* left me
Fallen trees, weak minds Chopped up concrete and everything nice

I left my fraudulent life between the A's and the B's written on our walls
I was the fittest, the smartest and the luckiest
Red burning blues in October never unnerved me I was unnerved anyways
I was a fraud anyways

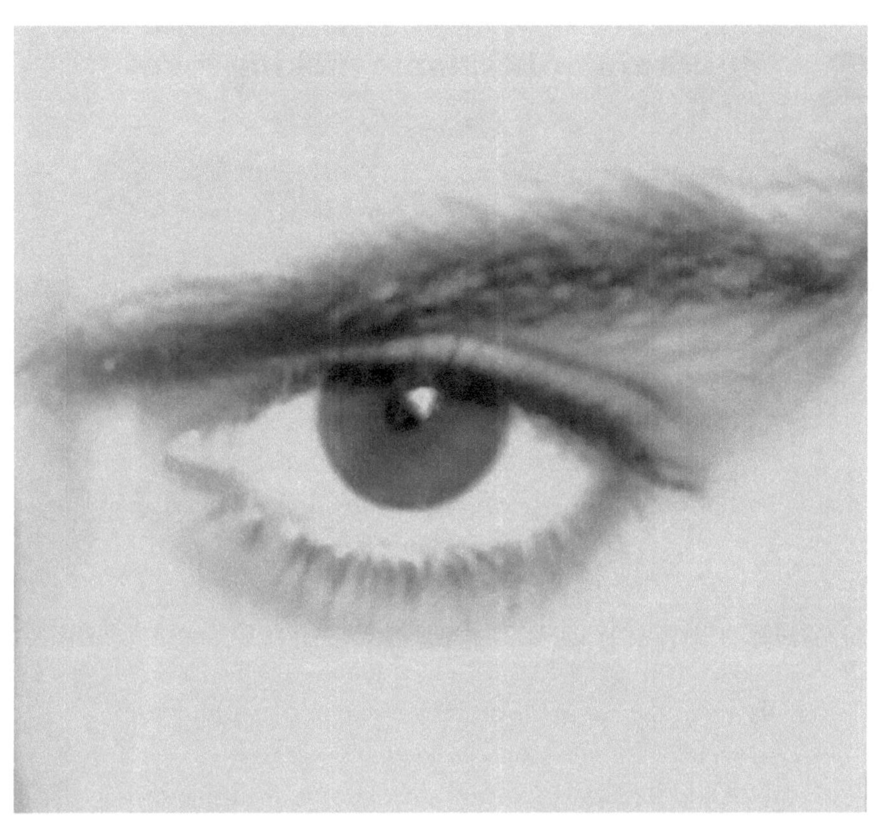

45

Jokes and jokes, lame fucking jokes

Hungry
Blood oozing out my nose and ears My eyes flooded, red tears
It was half past a gloomy noon I heard colors
And saw sounds
Steep hill, a fucking minefield of lame jokes And idiotic tantrums
What a fool I am
The best thing a girl can be in this world A beautiful fool
How the fuck am to climb? My wheels are worn out
And my limbs are red red red
I'm not above harming, killing and deflating my tires All because of your jokes
A minefield of triggers
When's your next spectacle if I may ask?
My birthday or yours My party or yours My funeral or yours Jokes and jokes
Lame fucking jokes
Is it you the spectacle or my array of poems about you?
The blood will stop for sure
And I'll have a picnic on the net of stars in the sky
Dream on and on
Forget your oath sworn to secrecy
And filled bellies

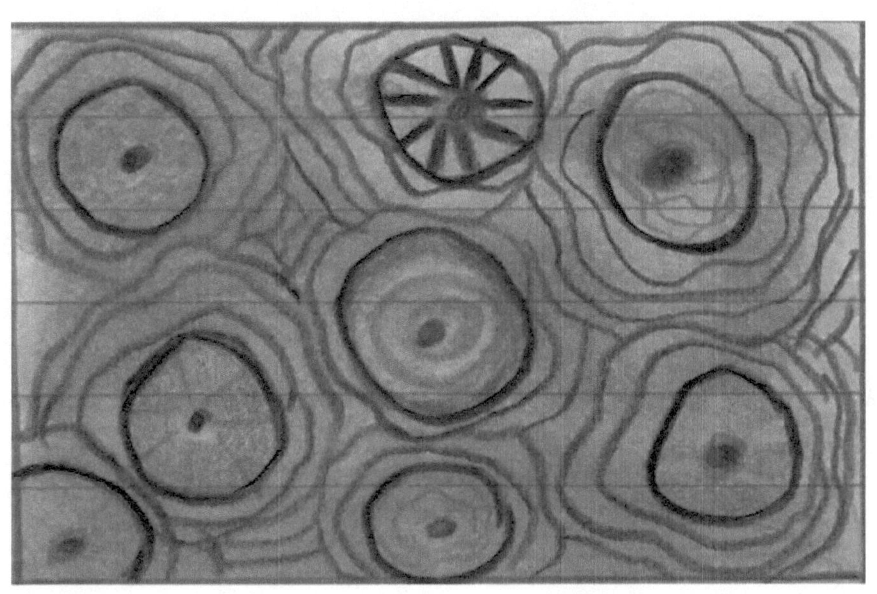

A bump in the road

I'm not an old soul
If anything, I'm a new one Nothing ever meant much to me Not cars from the fifties
Nor lovers in motels and under trees A bump in the road meant
For cars more than lives Will you remember this and that?
In death's lap
They taught you money and glory Wit and fame
Listening to the choir music about tales of true and glee Humming and teeth grinding
And unspoken pride that is dumb luck
A bump in the road for drunken sailors And their forgotten children from another lover
The bump is for their 2008 cars and
The plastic door handles and greasy steering wheels
In death's lap?
Will you remember this and that?
And shall you not crack under the weight of my mistakes My shortcomings
My fucking shortcomings
God's wraith
My wraith My Gods wraith
My wraith

I write to the fire, mother

I write in my beige walled kitchen And sometimes on the unwashed floor I
write to the fire, mother
Uproot my limbs from the yellow hued grass Move far far away where
Those men loving men And women loving women
Are devoted to worship my poetry Move far far away
To chambers where secrets are written on walls Of Gated dreams and withered
lashes

Green chalk And kohl of the east

Remove yourself from my windowsill, pretty please Jump for all I fucking care
Meet your death
Take your last fucking breath

I'll push you if I have to Then you'll meet my crossness Scream to
your lord almighty

Hoarse voice and all

Twice when you dare to defy my eyes And once when your skull
kisses your demise

I write to the fire, mother

I write to the fire about you

Thicker than water and thinner than blood

My brother raped a girl

Tore her nightgown at half past eleven Tears thicker than water
and thinner than blood Heart stronger than bones and weaker than
metal Hands softer than wood and sharper than leaves

And she leaves
Climbs out of the wild suburban trenches She leaves to the swan motel
Where sex was cheaper than a bag of apples And cops had the widows on their
knees She leaves him
He was her lover and her sailor Her baby daddy and jailor
Morbid fixation on her stupid eyes and nightly walks To get milk and eggs
Salt and vinegar
A virgin whose daddy left minutes after she was born from his addiction
Blame her soulless eyes with the dead nephew I've never met
Blame her mother who lost every fucking bet
Blame my brother's sick need to maim and wound
Or blame my mother, Grace

Therapy for the poor

It gets better when you want it to
My therapist tells me when she hears about the stories my mother And how
she gutted me and skinned my face
Wore my intestines with pride And shower it to my sisters on Eid She is a
mother I can tell

From the way she asks me to run Find a fucking husband and never
return And if I don't recognize my hair and voice

It only means I have made it

She never takes money from me Therapy for the poor and broken-hearted
Does she think I'm both?
Does she feel sorry for me and the womb I resided it For 9 months
I think she does but just on mornings noons and nights
She gently smiles when she reads my poems and says "you write about your
mother a lot"
But I only mention Grace once a poem Or maybe twice?
I never recall
But I recall her unconquerable voice telling me to pack my things and leave
Find love and follow my idiotic dreams
To drive as far as I can and never look in rearview mirror and see my mother
standing by the door to her house of cards
Fly away, little dove
All's well that ends well

All I'm saying

All I'm saying is
If your birthday shoes are too small Unclean
And tearing at the seams
Pack them and run unshod, unburdened and unhurt Put whiskey on your
scary blisters
Fresh meat and fresh wounds Count to three and count to four Count to three
and count to four Pack your bags
Close the door or leave it open, little girl

And they might say

Stick up to for your mother at all times Watch the sunrise around
dusk And the sunset around dawn

Believe in someone else's God as yours
Your deity
Bow and repeat *I worship thee* before sleep Read your fucking books and
magazines
And follow the directions on your phone screen
But in your heart of hearts
You know they're wrong and full of shit
So, play guitar downtown Algiers
And you'll be fine

Money boys and gowns

Bleached ego and coins Scattered in the pool of my tear The boys
and money stand by me

While I mourn enchanted relatives and their babies Good morning to the sun
and goodnight to the moon Good luck to me and goodbye to the scars
Goodbye to the boys and the gowns forced upon me The lace on the shoulders
and around my neck
Carrie I'm Carrie
Mary Bloody Mary
I just sit in my gown by the pool of my tears Drink tea and never mind
The bleached coins
The sun roasting my gown during the hours quiet When the party by the pool
ends
And Carrie carries the boy's plastic ring I carry my man's emerald ring
Dancing on my mother's shaded gravestone
My ego

In it, in the car

The weak perished and the strong ruled forevermore I must be the strong
Walk steadily and brave into my father's car Smile enough to feel my smile line
deepen Never deepen my plastic smile
Oh, what I would give to leave this place
Leave these pine trees on the side, trade them for maple trees
And I'm ashamed
But tell myself he loves me God loves me
Fine
Yet cigarettes, bad breaths and an unclean steering wheel Swimming with
other dirty cars
And unwashed glass, dust sits around home I have gone nose blind to the
smell
What I would give to leave this place
Not to Spain where mosques and cathedrals are one Or to Morocco where
they share my tongue
But sometimes the only way out is through

Anxiety

Be good and kind
Watch over them they're still babes
They scratch your face and stab your limbs And at night, they refuse to sleep
But be good and kind
Play with their hair and tickle them to tears Cuddle tight and let them hold
your index In their little hands, it fits perfect
Be good and kind
No more breeding adults with anxious souls Holding their thumbs to feel
secure
To feel safe, like you do To feel held, like you do
You thumb is fractured at times
Cause you hold too tight when your mother comes in Or when your sky is
crimson red
Vast and blinding, you can't even look
Be good and kind
So they don't break their bones
In search for an innocence, so long gone You lay in bed, muscles still and
compressed Like a lonesome stone in the desert
No rain or snow
just the scorching heat diurnal And the frosting cold nocturnal
No one hears the pounding in your chest No solace found, no glimpse of ease
Your bones quiver and your sky is crisp
You're forever lost within the undying eclipse
Your ears whistle to whomever shall help But it only echoes inside your chest
It's hot and cold
All you hold onto is your thumb
Maybe it's over you hope
Yet no sign of a guiding star, thus hope is afar Be good and kind

Other hearts may tremble to your words Watch over them they might be lost in the desert too

Just like you hoped someone watched over you

Me?

Orange thirteen

I think it's so beautiful that when we look at the sun, we all feel thirteen
We look into the distance and breathe in nostalgia For memories to come
And memories that were once Floating in the air, golden and free
Surrounding my mind with sweet daydreams As the sun shines through the clouds
The hues of orange and red dance across the sky That awaken love, a sight so grand
The memories rush into me of when I was thirteen When the sun's allure would sweep me of my feet Auroras touching every fibre of my spirit
Every ounce of lurk, shining light in it Memories, memories, memories
Slowly but unsurely the glimpse of my youth is dead The sun is no more thirteen and orange
In a sight beyond compare Painted by wings of artless angels Thirteen, a fleeting divine
I look up at fourteen
And I think it's so beautiful that when we look at the sun, we all feel thirteen

At the bay

I've crossed the street to avoid my nightmares
To avoid the clash between reality and hell
To avoid a conversation with my lonely neighbors But the grass grew between
the concrete stars

Where I buried my scarlet letters without a headstone The smell of
brokenness haunted me Followed me to school and to the bay

My godless feet run when the line was red Blue train and purple rains
The bay
The bay was on fire and my neighbors watched Sticking heads in windows of
white curtains And their whispers are loud and written in bold On my
forehead
Knuckles And lips
The waves, a scene from the notebook I found, burning the natural and
supernatural
No sense in speaking to scorned out fish Or gutted bees
Whom I sent to sweet poison the lady next door And sting the boy I was bent
my willow for The wind of their gossip won't mmm the fire The clouds of my
breath won't rain
The street was not to be crossed
Yet my rage blew out their candles and rattled their doors Shouting words that
infested in my guts
You will suffer my wrenching wraith You will share my tears in your death

Mad

All women become their mothers and that's their tragedy Yet love grows in
graveyards where I buried my selves Where I was once holy and pious
Then faithless and free
Recreated many selves that never resembled my mother's Dug my nails in my
chest, pulled my ribs to make new riffs For the music I shall dance to on the
grave of my last dress Did I escape you, mother?
Or am I becoming you? Dragging my agony around Sewn into every butterfly
that decorates my life
My tragedy is an ego made of sand So ambivalent and misled
Create Create
And create again
Birth to opinions and Medusa spirits
None echo my mother's thoughts or spineless judgements And when I avoid
my tragedy and walk into the uncharted And I wonder, mother
How long until someone walks into the premises and exposes my fraud My
oblivion
Mirror mirror on the wall
Am I my mother? Do I have her nose and eyes?
Or radiance and glam?

Hand-me-down

My father's hand-me-down anger and cruelty
It's too big and everyone can tell
The sleeves are long and the hem is worn out He worn it out
Stained the golden and green Set up spider nests in the back
Where flowers, unwatered, whither with no grace But when I sneeze, he shuts the hole in the
room Stuff it with his father's anger and agony
And it's vast, I get lost
And I know you bled and swam with the fishes Ran with wolves and guarded the sheep
Collected dust on your dreams
Or did you have any at all?
June to October November to May
I watch you smoke your ex-lover's last letter to you Stuff it with my mother's dried up leaves
Inhale harsh sorrows and exhale harsher sorrows Father, father, father
Will you put commas as you tell me the story
Or semicolons to tell me about the spiders' nest
Will you tell me that without me the world is just a floating rock in space Or will it be him?
He never yells because every time a man yells, I'm seven again
And I do, I do yell

He takes me to stand up comedies Where all the women laugh at their wounds

And all the men at their fathers

He holds my heart and never punctuates A lake with still waters is what he calls me

A divine stream made of forgetfulness, Lethe flows and heals Undresses me from hand me
downs
And gift me a water-colored dress To dance
And mend my bruised skin

To carry the legacy

I read a poem three or maybe two hours ago Or maybe a minute ago but I
don't recall
I can't
The words of little girls writing poetry at eighteen To write even more at
twenty-seven

And when they reach tapestry of their forties Where their wrinkles
grow like ivy on their foreheads

And blemishes on exposed skin No one reads their words anymore But I do
I do
"I come from a legacy of women
Who were raised to be useful
Rather than joyful"
I wonder if her mother loved and hated her like mine did Or if her father
broke her mother's spine like mine did Because my mother was useful too, I
swear
But her husband never ceased to glare!
I begrudge my father and my grandfather and his grandfather before him
For spilling boiling tea on their daughter's skin
Burning their flesh and dreams
And the little girls who once danced in sundresses at thirteen And chased bees
at noon
Are left with little hope and Holy fathers and broken spirits
Broken mothers and phantom dreams

She's here

My mother sat me next to the wooden desk The one she bought me
As a gift What a gift
A gift to keep on working to leave
But little does she know that I work to leave her Or maybe she knows
But she said I'm the worst she's ever had That her uterus is cursed to creating
me She tried to melt me and fucking piss me Like all the other sheddings of
her insides But I survived
She hit me with wooden spoon On my knuckles
Over And over
Until I uncovered my ears to hear She wanted me to hear
Some boiling anger resides in underneath my nails It was hot
Really hot
The AC broke and the heater is working overtime My love died that day
She died with it

Sleep walk

I sleep walk Blindly walk to the balcony

To hitch ride ghosts in our house
They roam and moan about their livelihood that was stolen Unfair
governments and corrupt politicians
They lure me with a cherished promise Sit on the edge of the window my love
Sit on the edge of the window my love Sit on the edge of the window my love I
do what they tell me
Fuck it, my father never holds me But ghosts do
My sisters say there are no ghosts And you shall catch a cold
No
Catch schizophrenia
It's contagious, or so she's heard
Our brother is schizophrenic and talks to the spoons The dishes and
sometimes to me
He once asked me "what's your name"
Where do you live and why are you on the cliff of our home
And my lovely sister is afraid my ghosts will fly me to the garden on the
mezzanine
I woke up to a gated balcony and boarded windows I sleep walk twice a month
Once on a full moon
And once on ... I don't remember
My ghosts say there's light in my eyes, unconquerable solitude
But I know gated balconies will stop my ghosts My ghosts
Mine

I want out, out of my mind

Blues Jazz Yellows Indie
Sensual smiles across streets
Don't look at me
Not now
I want out, out of my mind
Out, slipping between the black and white screen
At nineteen o'clock
I have dreams
About another me in a starship, abiding to God's will Abiding to the sun
burning through my will and hers There are trains and tunnels with no light
My mind's made up of trains and tunnels with no light My mind's rigid
dimmed colors and my mother's memory With my father's hands
I hate it up there but it's mine till the stars' fading reaches
Mine, all mine

I talk about me a lot, I know Little do I see when my mother touches

Something about her dry hands touching mine sends Snakes crawling down
my spine
Up my spine Down my spine
Two seconds and a few thousand more I see it all
I want out, out of my mind

Your mother and mine

You're so handsome and kind
Your mother is unlike mine Twice as patient and twice as sweet

Bathe me clean from my mother's kisses Cleanse my ears from my sister's worst
In a sea where adventurers sailed away From their mothers and fathers
Wash away my withering bones And wake me
Wake me, love and remind me of who I'm supposed to be
Sew my wound shut in the Red Sea
God knows no one cut the wounds on my wrists But my own hands every
scary night
And don't be afraid to skin my back from my unhappy
the wound from my daddy
Too young to marry, too old to swim Too young to sail, too ardent to die But
too tired to leave
Strap me on your back with my torn-up clothes Carry my weight and yours
Like your mother carried hers and yours

R.I.P

Summer, is that you?

Summer, is that you?
Summer sunrise Forest pool Meadows of the age
Meadows of the ancient age Intertwined branches of love And beaches of
green
Hushed gossip of the pine trees Saluting the living and the dead And everyone
in between
The sick and the healthy The poor and the wealthy
Beach summer and forest summer, unalike One is cold
One is dark
She bowed to the willows and the leaves silk and green She is summer
She is noon She is rage
She is a forest fire Unplanned
Summer, is that you?

Pancakes

She taught me to make pancakes Sugar and more sugar
Lemon zest and lemon zest Sixteen, sweet baby sixteen with baby
skin

Bright under eyes
Ready to conquer the mall with interlocked hands and open hearts Now I do
have an open heart
Acid seeping and seeping through
Now we're on the same ride home and act like strangers Stranger fucking
danger
A lump in my throat sits and enlarges as we avoid eyes Sweet little girl, doe
eyed mean girl
I remember when you told me to mix eggs with love Serve it with jam and a
joke
Everything about this car looks like it's 1979
The windshield and the rear-view mirror We wanted one, do you recall?
Do you recall?

Lemon ice cream and parking lot jokes Too wild to believe in a
suburban life in Algiers

I do recall though, I do
We were on death row since we met Waiting for doomsday; October 2018

I was afraid I would be another statistic

When Grace whispers in the ears of her own children Her little men she so
fiercely screamed into this earth Tells them my nail polish is why I should be
hurt Grace loves me sometimes
But not all the time
Grace is my mother Hence the name The tears
And the hair The soft skin The Dry skin And nails
Mother oh mother
I don't wish for my nails to be as dry as yours
Or my hair as brown as yours
I want them to be soft like Snow White's
And I want my skin to be like hers Day and night
And when I find a whole hearted man
I will make him buy me all the lavish gifts and clothes All them remedies and
gels
To soften up my skin and hide my scars That your little soldiers gave me
On Fridays and Saturdays at first
Grace, oh Grace My grace my grace
Remember when your fucking bipolar mind told me I wasn't worth anything
Or when your worthless boys told you I deserved the pain Well guess what?
I won't be another statistic, another dead daughter But you will be one,
another bad mother

Rue me rue me rue me

It's a quarter past four
Past when I lost my novelty
When my mentor told me I'm bullet proof and love proof.
And I read between the words and the silent letters Why you rue the day I saw
your scars
And poet to poet
Do you fantasize about it at noon
When the streets are beaming and humming my name
My sworn enemies' and nonchalant friends'
About a simple life with a husband your brother chose I see you and you see
me
I am you; you are me
Do you hear my voice when you're falling asleep Living in the chasm between
your empathy and mine Scroll it away

Scroll away Scroll it all away Scroll myself away Scroll my life away

Art and men

For Valentine's Day I thought I would buy a gun
But I actually bought two
One in my closet and one on your forehead A self-proclaimed man's forehead
First impressions and niceties
I'm an ally cat and you talk about me day and night
Night and day
You drive me fucking insane
And I'm in no mood to play games today
But I will carve my name on your back with a dull blade And sing aloud all my
disgust and explain
Why do I bother to explain?
To translate my convictions into digestible texts Read it once and it is funny

Read it twice and it is cruel Read it thrice and it is blasphemy

It is art to me But you're just a man Come to me in need

Come and tell me how to hurt myself Every breath is a sudden death
around your ego

I'm not afraid to disfigure and ruin the

Clover fields and wild flowers Dig your grave with my bare hands

Your hands on your heart and spoiled soul Your soul; your vanity
But I do hope you enjoy my bullets of truth My bullets of lies
My bullets on Valentine's Day

I need a mechanic

Is that weird?
That it took everything in me My teeth and my neurons
Not to leave the car in the middle of traffic 6AM traffic

Break the windshield and the engine Pour gasoline and set it on fire
Sit on the midst of the highway

My highway
The government's highway?
But I do it anyways, fuck my teeth and neurons I sit and watch the cars pass by
me
On my left and on my right On my right and on my left
But I don't mind and I don't care
Free show for the mindless and the scared Will they pay next time?
To see the worst of me
Sticks and stones always broke my bones
So now I'm on very legal drugs
Legal drugs, legal I swear
But people drive by and no one stares at the mess that I am
The product of my father's present absence And my mother's absent presence
Is that weird?
That my anger speeds up when I look up to the sky Where my heart is parked
by smallest cloud
That diesel leaks from my eyes and leaves a trail on my cheeks Is that weird?
That I need a mechanic?

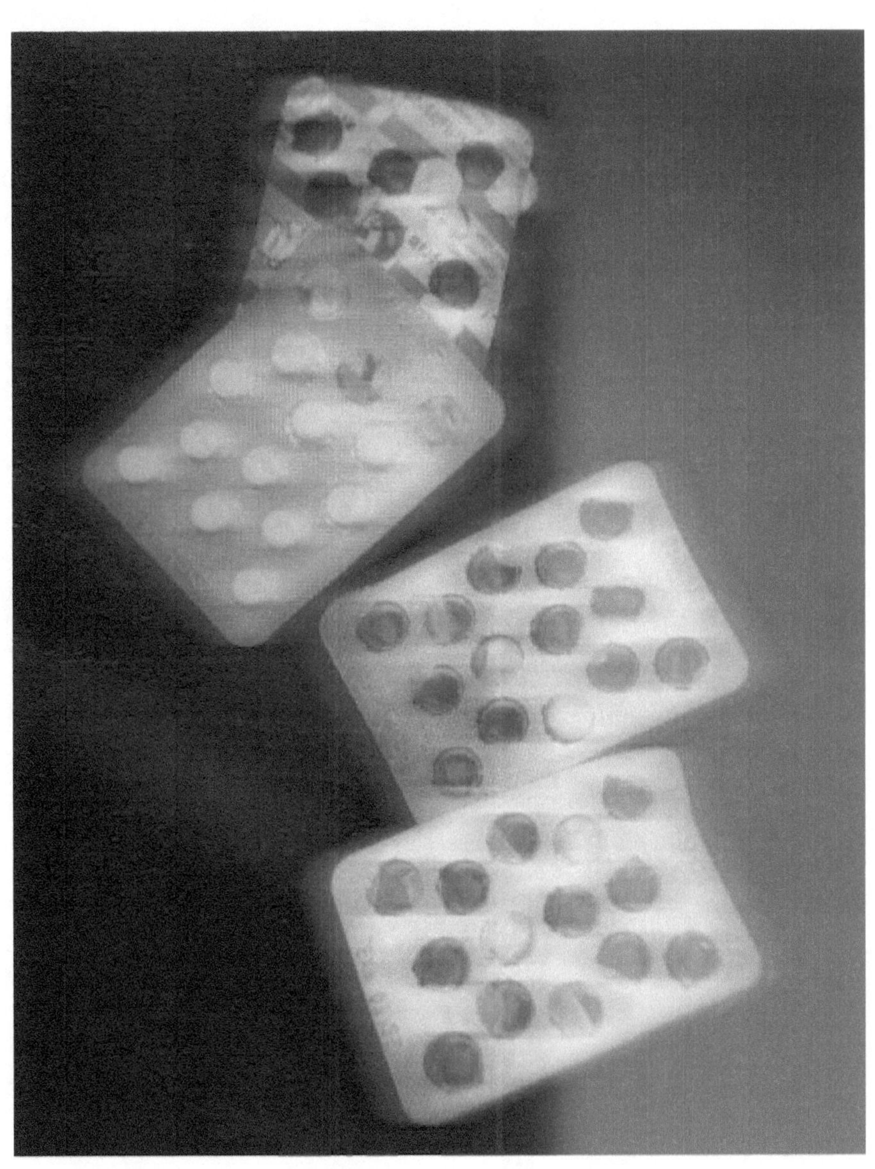

Emails

A few mails ago with an open heart
I looked out the window and saw the gates open The gates of heavens and hell
Screamed to the artless angels with a force of fire Do you remember my name?
I was once like you
But my parents fought too loud With my mother's auto tuned cries And my
father's untuned attention I drank the lake to sober up
Shoved grass in my ears to never hear their polished lies I hid behind the
overly painted door
That had my brother's jacket from before he went to jail
I spoke to the creeks that let the light in And kept the pain out
I was once like you!
But my father picked on my feathers He thought my wings were too blue Too
burning blue
Or maybe too fragile? I do not remember
I do not wish to remember how you cried when I was gone And rained my
town with your sharpened tears
You hoped for my quick return
That mail, drove my mother to tears, she dropped her heart and I heard it
break
I woke up screaming "take me home"
But I was, home.

Mentor

When schools were churches and mosques Holy gatherings and harsh mentors
My mentor made my efforts to arrive seem Monumental achievements
Glory of years to behold
She liked my poetry and seasons that broke my back
My lover's and my friends'
Poems written when I was bored if I let go of lying in my poems about Bentley
and Bugatti
About Harvard and Harvard
I admire her dedication to secrecy and privacy My unaccepted friend requests
on Facebook
I admire how she talks to God like I do Scared and scared
As if the earth would open and swallow her whole But it might, right?
Unborn fear
Like a smudge that won't budge Even if it's on an angel's wing
But at least she opens her eyes at dawn and think of us, of me
"You will write the next best poetry book" she believes
But I do not hope so
I hope no one reads and no one sees

Guns in my closet

Keeping guns in my closet
Pink dresses, below the knee and above my brother's ego
Sweaty grip, bathed in my blood My firearm
My right arm
Standing at bother ends of the barrels at all times I shall be my own your own
foe
My own friend lying
Shall these boards bear witness of Skeletons of past
Skeletons of present Spilled guts on your floor
In meadows of irises and poisonous weed Greenery holds snakes
Homely closets holding guns
My vanity My sanity
In meadows of irises and poisonous weed Greenery holds snakes
Homely closets holding guns No one knows
Bored of Independence Day and birthdays

When I'm done, I'm gone

I smoked once or twice our champagne forest Rolled the leaves and the weeds
In a limo behind our neighbors shed
Broken the shed and cracked the ground beneath my bare feet Burnt his house
down
Independent of his jokes and lifeless friends No one will be left to know the
old me
The gone me
No faith me, not in humanity or me Or God
Violets by the edge of the forest I pick them up one by one
Root and fucking stem, root and fucking stem Sit and digest the petals
A star imploding A star absorbing
I lie
I say I don't have faith in God anymore

But I do I do Who am I kidding?

Ad Astra Per Aspera

Rough roads lead to the stars Rough upbringings lead to bumpy roads Stolen mothers and kidnapped babies

Barbed wires My barbed wire
Armies and independence jokes past their prime Past their truth
For the sunny weather family
Who tells me to sleep off the pain of my unmittened hands Unshoed feet
And uncovered head
Sleep it off, we'll be there before you know it We'd reach the stars and travel to
Mars
And yes yes yes
I've always known I would sleep more than most I've always known I would
miss the shooting stars And how funny
When I was a kid
I used to think snow was a myth Until I walked down the aisle To the stars

I don't want to live in Copenhagen

I don't want to live in Copenhagen
Pretty apple pie
I don't want to live in Calgary Pretty apple pie

I want I want I don't

I want to roam the street of Algiers Where trees are squares

And the leaves are forever green Greener than my eyes in pretentious
settings

Where people never play fair

Busy streets and police patrolling my ego They were navy blue and baby blue
Riviera sand and Mediterranean hues French castles and light truths
Not too heavy on my heart
A complex creature aiming to belong To a nation
To an entity of pride
Kiss better my dreams Knit me a sweater of hope To warm my pale truth
And my nights in Copenhagen or Algiers Calgary or Ciamis

A Bentley in Algiers

The clock wouldn't go faster
Nor my mind slower
I wrote a poem in my head before sleep Then I wrote another
I memorized the creeks between the vowels Counted the numbers and
mistakes
I memorized all my dull jokes and rhetoric metaphors And my Victorian
questions
No No
I memorized all my dull jokes and Victorian metaphors And my rhetoric
questions
I wrote a poem in my head before sleep
About my professor's microphone in our blue amphitheatre
My humiliation device and comedic love I slow dance with a bully I shall not
name Touch or plague
But I distract my lowly mind and count again Oceans of cars; I count the
German and the French The wealthy and the Bentley
Algerian heroes and namely me Counting vowels and cars in Algiers In my
bed, before sleep

0297691851 6

Amsterdam

Walking the streets of Amsterdam Afraid they'd know where I'm from I don't wear green or red

And if I do, I never add white But what a shame it is to be ashamed

Fear resides in my heart, locking a secret In this ethereal city where diamonds shine Never dim in day or night
The space between the rocks on the ground Where my ghost follows me and hide
Amsterdam or in the depths of the heart of Greece Their gaze scorns my barbarian nose
up and down They know They know
Whispers of high self-esteem, a purer race?
Or a claim of borders and lines
The scarf whether it's white, red or green
Belonging to the other side of the sea
But parts of me drowned then and I'm drowning now
Are they laughing at my walk? Or the way I talk?
My brown eyes or my sharpened teeth Shame on the colors that bred fear Fear of being known in Amsterdam

Forever a sponge

Deflate, my darling love Breathe in and out
Let the toxins pour out of your doe eyes Sleep in the day
Ignore that funny feeling
You're fine okay
Your tears are crystals and your jewels are made of tins But no one understands
and I do
I do I do
Your boyfriend's kind and never smoke or drink
His lungs are fine And so are yours

Just ignore the fire and the smoke no one sees No one sees that you're
not okay Noxious spirit with a heavy gas

Spill your brains on the table but no one eats But he does

And I do I do
I do

You're like a sponge, cleaning a mess of their making Drink in their
tears and their bashing words You're like a ghost, your eyes and
ambition

Fly away my butterfly You'll be okay far away I'm sorry love
For damaging your sight and leaves

At last

My dreams are spiralling out of hand At night, I wander off to foreign land
The murals, splintered and filled with doubt And with utter sorrow, silver
eagles shout In old suburban times are my dreams Where the houses shatter at
the seams Holding back demons that dance in glee Heinous and wishing to be
an escapee
The roofs are pictures of the yellow sand Where scorpions fly and I don't
understand Why mother is wearing white
Faceless running out with fright
And why the twelfth bed begrudges the sleeper Soaking his colors in, then
spiting him out a weeper The drums of my heart are faint and lean
Few and far in between
And everything is not what it seems to be Lost in this cynical perpetuity

Strange

Standing at the elementary school Haunting bullies and cruel teachers Staring
at where recess started
The yard where I fell at nine

And the kids, like little demons surrounding me Looking down to
me, and I'm in a grave Haunting that school yard, my graveyard
Their laughs are muffled, far and strange

I look up and my small-town dreams rise Softly shush my fears
Kiss my forehead, a farewell from hell
I'm a shapeless ghost, floating through the suburbs

Diving into my morning memories Elementary school then hospital
where I was born

My father, kind and cruel Plucked a pure fresh heart
Made it into an anxious broken heart So, cars crash

And birds fall Trains derail And people die

Buried at nine and at 3 hours old A shapeless ghost is all I am
Haunting all that made me what I am

Like a fish in a bowl

Swim little me
It hurts now because you are afraid of everything The water and the salt
Your eyes burn and your knees are weak You admit your unrelenting hypocrisy
About women's rights and your mother's rights
Swim little me
Look up to the sky and watch the fireworks Unknown sources
Or could it be my heart erupting at last? You sense it all, the smoke and the
water The smoke in your lungs
The water in your lungs
Will your body burn out or sail away?
Swim little me
Look up to the sky and watch a holiday You are not acquainted with
You are not acquainted with seabirds circling above your head Shrieking
Sharks and sharks below your feet Sharks and sharks
And what a damn shame it is All this splashing and drinking And you're still
sober and aware Drink the whole ocean
Drink the whole bowl
I'm not a shark, I am a koi fish
Not in an ocean In a fishbowl

Sweet tears

If I cry about it, it means it's real
If I let my broken spine shiver And my hoard the truths inside my liver

Then it means it's real
I watched blue irises wither away in spring Marry limbs; who pick their petals away One
After One
Marry to collect their nonchalance behind them And polish their cutlery when they go mad
Listen as they call another woman's name in their sleep
And on afternoons like these
When the oaks sing for my sisters' pain
A lullaby, humming their cries away I carry within me my sad mother And her mother
And her mother before her

I hear my bones creaking under their weight A plethora of years of shame, tears and
suffering

Clogging their air in the open space On moors of ripe grains of sorrows My heart remembers
For days and decades
And I pray daisies grow in the saddest parts of their heart And tulips in their darkest
memories

Asymmetrical

God and Prada Life and the afterlife
Now and then 2002 to quarantine
I wonder why you loathe hourly Hourly paid to wear a mask, avoid
ill health

Avoid me
A storm in the sky merged with the *whatever* sea No lines or limits
No clear skyline to separate the good from The bad
I see it all now
I'm well aware now
That the depth of the waters doesn't mean wisdom And the height of the sky
doesn't mean pride Wisdom and pride mustn't fuse
Asymmetrical faces and misaligned wrinkles A crooked crown, a crooked nose
Breeds an ego from a pride A tumour from a stroke
My unshod feet bleed, no Prada or a man

A good sinner

Don't speak unless you're spoken to Don't look unless you're looked at And
never smile first
My mother repeats before guests arrive
I hate to disappoint her and tell her the truth
That I'm no good at any of that
That I break her rules every single time Without fail
I never fail at sinning and breaking the law All I am is a good sinner
I will never understand my obsession My morbid fixation with uncut emeralds
While my friends talk all about their fathers' favourite lemon cakes
And how the crumbs mix with the cream While the butter melts
They talk and talk and I know what it is
I know what it is and I wish I could feel the same stars in my heart Sparking
every time my father talks
Because that's what they are to me
Stars
Untouchable and unavailable to me since 2002

And I could never be good with prayers A good daughter
A good sister And a good worshiper But I *am* a good sinner

I hate to die and all that's left of me is my offspring
Who will die too That's why I write I think

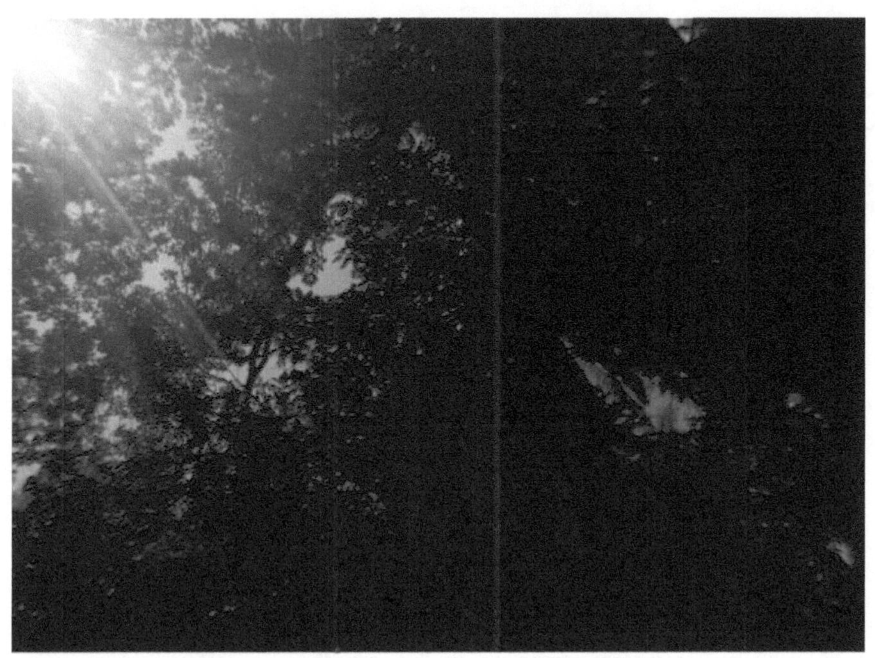

Slow snow

The clock ticked my death, when the car flew on the highway Spirits laugh and kiss
Ghostly, their eyes forever on the abyss Wondering who the new one might be
Dreams dream to be mine
Slowing the traffic to the heavens
The gates, artless within the realms of nothingness And refuge is my tomb of untold ornery secrets
Where snow sways with the winds and never bends to the truth My eclipsed spirit curses the bitterness of my blood
As it colors the snow, the slow snow The horizon, where is hope?
I stand and look around at my numb breath Mother, grandmother and great-grandmother Haul my spirit away
"Hush hush my love", yet I scream
Take me where sinners bound to break the forsaken oath Where the promised lands shall forever hold
Take me where thinking in riddles is certain and sincere Mother, am I gone?
Father, am I insane? Lover, am I in love?
Pale decorum and ancient teachings Am I with you or with ungodly beings?

Happy birthday, happy Valentine's Day, happy Independence Day ... etc

Happy birthday, little angel
Today you're born and tomorrow you die A baby will you always be

Always changing into the new The new thought and doctrine of faith

So dramatic
And when they call you dramatic, it fucking hurts And it never shows
Why do you cry on your birthday, little love Little love do you have?

Crowded heartbeats and low on life While strangers watch and admire your smile

Your poems and made-up words
Happy Valentine's Day, my little lovebuzz Would you believe me when I tell you You're the queen of my heart
My heartstrings and abyss of love
The next best poet in Algiers and the whole small world Happy Independence Day, little bird
Today you fight and tomorrow you rest Rest in peace beneath where we used to run Roots that dive in the bottomless
You hate the never ending and the endless You fear life and death
You cry on your birthday, Valentine's Day and Independence Day

History

I wish I could say I am on the right side of history That I protested day and
night
But I did not
But I would say I stayed home on October November
December And January

And every other fucking month that follows Where the living keep
on dying Where the dead keep on dying

I cracked a can of coke at 7AM And I know
I know
An hour ahead, in forbidden streets and inhabited buildings Cracked skulls
and peaking bones
Bloody sidewalks and decomposed bodies At the altar of the oppressor
They offer their eyeballs and offspring Sacrifice dreams and love
And I am a woman at home watching Watching
Cold conversation with the press That presses on wounds
And I wonder how it feels to die for your land Your home
Home
I would leave home
The cracks of my heart are because of my home
And if you ever wonder if the cold air seeps in between the cracks It does

Wine or water?

My sister occasionally sips on my empathy Open windows and hollow walls
Containing angry conversations and shallow thoughts Yes or no, I need an
answer
Love me or leave me, I need an answer
But your eyes bleed on your shoulder where I used to lay my head

I'm bad and good And you're bad and bad

Little can my spits do when the drought begins And the bad overweighs the
good
The bad overpowers what's been done
And what could be done But I slept twice today
Or took a few million naps that would never replenish my youth Or the dead
skin underneath my eyes
Or the wild neurons inside my brain Is it you, sister?
Or is it mother?
I know she spilled her sorrows in her milk and now it's in your bones and mine
A bipolar mind, a dual heart and stiff fingers That could never write a letter, let
alone a poem But I write
I write your scars away in an ink that never runs out And when it does
I use our shared blood
And that's how you sip on my empathy

My blood and neurons But is it water to you, or wine?

Freedom of the dead and the living and everything in between

It's October 2023
No No
It's November 3rd, 2023
And the hurt and lonely are counting stars But when I look up, I see ravens
In an eerie glow in the sky
So, I go online and watch missiles and wars Skies raining deaths and more and
more
A teddy bear sat on rubble and rotten limbs In desolate land, the lonely ghosts
shrieked It belonged to another girl
Who died at thirteen
Up up up from a sweet sweet dream
People were chanting her name on glorious protests No, they were chanting a
pop star's name
For her beauty and fame
But it's a sweet sweet dream
Where freedom of the dead and the living and everything in between Lies in
the hand of an evil man
Oh, evil men

Airports at 6 o'clock

The airports light up at 6 o'clock and I dream of leaving
Heavy glittery heart, safe and sound
And mauve skies and not for the sake of poetic metaphors I swear on my life
On my lifetime of achievement And polite regards
On my father's love And Grace's joy
In my gardens of Babylon
Airports are veins within the violets, late autumn all through spring Birds sit
by lakes of my fears and whisper
Schemes
And surmise, by the look of me
That I'm a fucking coward But I'm not
I am not
I can't be fearless
But I promise I can be unafraid
Never mind, mindless birds All my clouds are raining acid On field of pine
trees
And queer uprooted violets
It's the cost of the things I shall see
Survive to be tall again like pine trees
But airports in the frost of 6 o'clocks
And 7 AMs
Cause me irregular dreams
Where the storm ends when the plane lands On a barren land

My sun and my moon

I don't begrudge the sun, protector of our realm
I don't begrudge the moon, commander of the sea and oceans
But I do the rains softly seeping into your skin No umbrella, you hate and love
the rain
A complex creature, with a gap between your teeth With a fire in your eyes
And a feathery heart of glass
A lonesome night, that shaped you into a man When daffodils withered, yet
your patience thrived A slow walker, short steps and smiles in between Warm
breaths, clouds of never-ending purity Lasting wisdom and maturity
And when the trees and birds sing together no more And the grass is no longer
vibrant green
An apocalyptic scene
My compass will lead me to you
My lifeline shall perish all the way through
That's when you know I love you

Fate intertwined

We've always been connected
Weirdly connected and you know fucking it
Like when we have the same dream on the same night before dawn Like how
we had an accident at the same of the day miles apart Like how in our little
book club
We choice the same books It is fate
It is providence Is it not?
You say that mars is within my reach and even the other planets You say that
my poems will go down in history
But I don't
I hope no one reads or sees
I let go but when I do I look around Maybe like *they* say
You only get what you want when you *let go* The paint only dries when you
stop watching it The grass only grows when you're not around
Your connection only fades when you stop listening And I listen
I do
I hear the humming of Mars And how fate intertwines

Music to my eyes

It is 5:01
The sun is in countries I cannot visit
Venture in their alleys of history and tormented cultures Tormented youth
and scarred culture
Listening to the song you made for me Your only Goddess Aphrodite
The girl with crooked teeth and two left feet Stolen rings and stolen roots
Not Arab Not African
Not European for sure
The idiocy of your love and mine are not for the faintest of hearts It is
crushing belief
It is banality at 5.01 And novelty at 17.01
The remnants of normality we can never have rendered us defeated Thrown
like a cigarette butt
But love love love
You put my mother's love to shame
You read the newspaper and understand women like me That a woman like me
thinks and sleeps more than most I just want to live and die
And that is the best thing a woman can ask for these days Goodbye sun

Goodbye moon Good morning, Saturn
Goodnight at noon

Four cold hands

Four cold hands Two holding each other

Four worn out shoes Two pink and two blue Four brown eyes
Two fear it all and two don't

Five shirts and a hoodie on top Ninety three percent polyester and
six cotton

That other one percent is tears and bleach I remember the counting
One two three steps One two three blinks
They call it OCD but does a crippled home really give you that?
I could have asked when I was nine or thirteen Twenty or sweet sixteen
But my questions always went unanswered

Four cold hands Two holding each other

Four worn out shoes Two pink and two blue Four brown eyes
Two fear it all and two don't
Dirty hand-me down converse from my best friend's kind mother
Unwashed light jeans
Yours were too big and mine were too small I remember the nails biting
Right hand first, my thumb first then my index Left hand second, my thumb
first then my index
They call it anxiety, but does a crippled home really give you that?
I should have never asked back when I was nineteen Cause usually my
questions always go unanswered
Now this perfume smells like a time I don't recall This room stinks of a joy that
I don't have

And these scars in my hand speak about a family I don't love
anymore

April is a pen name for Maroua Koriba.

November 1st Avenue is a collection of poetry about family, anger, religion, abuse. Every poem is a story and every photograph mirrors it.